DISASTER ZONE
ICE STORMS

by Vanessa Black

po_g_o

Ideas for Parents and Teachers

Pogo Books let children practice reading informational text while introducing them to nonfiction features such as headings, labels, sidebars, maps, and diagrams, as well as a table of contents, glossary, and index.

Carefully leveled text with a strong photo match offers early fluent readers the support they need to succeed.

Before Reading

- "Walk" through the book and point out the various nonfiction features. Ask the student what purpose each feature serves.
- Look at the glossary together. Read and discuss the words.

Read the Book

- Have the child read the book independently.
- Invite him or her to list questions that arise from reading.

After Reading

- Discuss the child's questions. Talk about how he or she might find answers to those questions.
- Prompt the child to think more. Ask: Have you ever experienced an ice storm? Were you prepared?

Pogo Books are published by Jump!
5357 Penn Avenue South
Minneapolis, MN 55419
www.jumplibrary.com

Library of Congress Cataloging-in-Publication Data

Names: Black, Vanessa, author. | Black, Vanessa. Disaster zone.
Title: Ice storms: disaster zone / by Vanessa Black.
Description: Minneapolis, MN: Jump!, Inc. [2017]
Series: Disaster zone
Audience: Ages 7-10. | Includes bibliographical references and index.
Identifiers: LCCN 2016005781 (print)
LCCN 2016006257 (ebook)
ISBN 9781620313992 (hardcover: alk. paper)
ISBN 9781624964466 (ebook)
Subjects: LCSH: Ice storms—Juvenile literature.
Winter storms—Juvenile literature.
Classification: LCC QC926.37.B53 2017 (print)
LCC QC926.37 (ebook) | DDC 551.55/6—dc23
LC record available at http://lccn.loc.gov/2016005781

Series Editor: Jenny Fretland VanVoorst
Series Designer: Anna Peterson
Photo Researcher: Anna Peterson

Photo Credits: Corbis, 8-9, 10-11, 15; Getty, 4, 6-7, 12-13, 16-17, 19; iStock, cover; Shutterstock, 1, 3, 5, 14, 18, 23; Thinkstock, 20-21.

Printed in the United States of America at Corporate Graphics in North Mankato, Minnesota.

TABLE OF CONTENTS

CHAPTER 1

IT'S AN ICE STORM!

It has been raining all day. But now the raindrops are turning into ice as they hit the ground. The sidewalk is so slippery you cannot walk.

Roads are ice rinks.
Cars skid out of control.
It's an ice storm!

Forecasters hope the **weather pattern** will change soon. But for now, it seems to be holding. Freezing rain falls and falls. Everything is coated in ice. Tree branches break. Power lines get heavy and **collapse**.

Emergency workers try to help, but roads are piled with crashes. It's hard to get anywhere.

DID YOU KNOW?

A half inch (1.3 centimeters) of ice on power lines can equal 500 pounds (227 kilograms)!

Freezing rain occurs when a warm layer of air sits above a cold, **shallow** layer. Rain forms in the warm layer. When the rain falls through the cold layer, it cools. The rain does not turn to snow or ice. It stays a liquid. But when it hits a cold surface, it instantly freezes.

TAKE A LOOK!

Water vapor in the clouds turns to rain and then ice when it touches something cold.

■ = warm air ■ = cold air

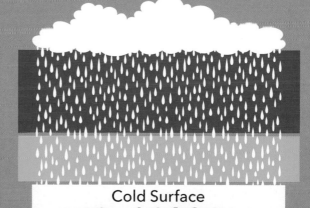

Cold Surface

The ice storm gets worse.
The Internet is down.
So are the phone lines.
More and more people
lose power. Without power,
homes get cold. It is an
emergency!

DID YOU KNOW?

When it is cold, wear a hat!
As much as 50 percent
of your body heat is lost
through your head.

Finally, the freezing rain stops.
But everything is still coated in ice.
Workers put salt on the roads to help
melt the ice. But the ice is so thick,
it takes days for the roads to be cleared.
Slowly, workers fix the power lines.
Heat returns to homes.

WHERE DO THEY HAPPEN?

Most ice storms in the United States occur in the Midwest and the Northeast.

UNITED STATES

☐ = Ice Storm Zones

CHAPTER 2

DEADLY ICE STORMS

In January 1998, an ice storm hit Quebec, Canada. The storm caused billions of dollars in damage. The maple syrup **industry** was especially hurt. Millions of maple trees were **destroyed** by ice.

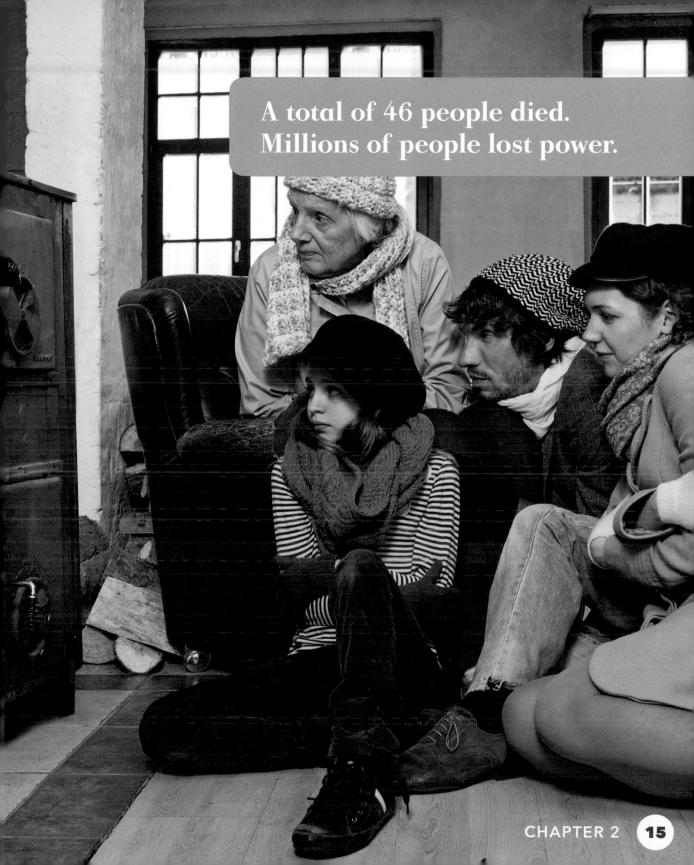

A total of 46 people died.
Millions of people lost power.

In January 2000, an ice storm in Atlanta, Georgia, caused problems for Super Bowl XXXIV. About 500,000 people were without power. Stores and restaurants could not stay open. Some places did not have power for over a week! Then, just as the ice storm was clearing, Atlanta got smacked with a snowstorm. The roads were very bad. The teams couldn't even make it to the **dome** to practice!

CHAPTER 3

STAYING SAFE

Ice storms are dangerous. People fall and break bones. Cars crash. Tree branches break.

Power poles crack. Power lines fall. Homes get very cold. People suffer from **hypothermia**.

ACTIVITIES & TOOLS

MELTING ICE

Can you melt an ice cube without changing the temperature? Let's see!

You will need:
- two ice cubes of the same size
- salt

❶ First, place two ice cubes on a plate.

❷ Measure out two large pinches of salt.

❸ Sprinkle the salt on one of the ice cubes.

❹ Watch and observe: Which ice cube melts first?

Why does this work?

Salt lowers the freezing point of water. That's why salt is put on roads to help melt ice.

collapse: To fall down.

destroyed: Ruined.

dome: An arena that is covered with a roof shaped like half of a golf ball.

emergency: An unexpected situation that calls for immediate action.

forecasters: People who predict the weather.

hypothermia: When a person's body temperature gets very low.

industry: A group of businesses that make the same thing.

shallow: Not deep.

water vapor: Water in its gaseous state, especially when below boiling temperature and spread through the atmosphere.

weather pattern: A term used to talk about what the weather is doing over a period of time.

INDEX

TO LEARN MORE

Learning more is as easy as 1, 2, 3.

1) **Go to www.factsurfer.com**

2) **Enter "icestorms" into the search box.**

3) **Click the "Surf" button to see a list of websites.**

With factsurfer, finding more information is just a click away.